Published in 2014 by The Rosen Publishing Group, Inc.
29 East 21st Street, New York, NY 10010

Adaptations to North American Edition © 2014 by The Rosen Publishing Group, Inc.
Copyright © 2014 Axis Books Limited

First Edition

US Editor: Joshua Shadowens

Library of Congress Cataloging-in-Publication Data

Bolitho, Mark.
 Fold your own origami navy / by Mark Bolitho. — First edition.
     pages cm. — (Origami army)
 Includes index.
 ISBN 978-1-4777-1318-1 (library binding) — ISBN 978-1-4777-1467-6 (paperback) —
 ISBN 978-1-4777-1468-3 (6-pack)
 1. Origami—Juvenile literature. 2. Military miniatures—Juvenile literature. 3. Navies—Miscellanea—Juvenile literature. I.
Title.
 TT872.5.B655 2014
 736'.982—dc23
                                          2013005112

Manufactured in the United States of America

CPSIA Compliance Information: Batch #S13PK8: For Further Information contact Rosen Publishing, New York, New York at 1-800-237-9932

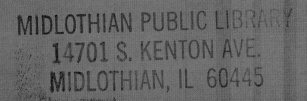

Origami
ARMY

Fold Your Own ORIGAMI
NAVY

Mark Bolitho

PowerKiDS
press
New York

CONTENTS

INTRODUCTION

Did you ever think you could make a **submarine** or aircraft carrier from pieces of paper? With accurate instructions and techniques there's no end to what can be made using **origami**. Origami is the ancient art of folding paper to make models. It has been popular in Japan for hundreds of years. The word *ori* means "folding," and *kami* means "paper."

The United States Navy is the largest navy in the world. It is bigger than the next 13 largest navies combined! The navy uses its ships to protect the US from threats by sea. The navy traces it origins back to the **American Revolution** when the Continental Navy was formed on October 13, 1775. The navy has over 300,000 active duty **personnel** and over 100,000 reserve personnel.

There are many different career paths within the US Navy. One is an elite force called the Navy SEALs. SEALs are used for special **reconnaissance** or defense missions. A group of SEALs was responsible for finding the terrorist Osama bin Laden in Pakistan.

This book will take you through five fun origami projects inspired by the US Navy. You will begin by learning about materials and techniques that will help you be successful with your projects. Just follow the instructions, and you'll soon have you own **fleet** of paper masterpieces!

MATERIALS AND EQUIPMENT

All the projects in this book are made from square or rectangular pieces of paper. Here are the basic tools you need, and instructions for getting your paper to the right **proportions**.

All you really need is a pair of hands and a piece of paper. To achieve the best results keeps your hands clean, and use your fingers to manipulate the paper: enhance the creases using fingertips and nails.

CHOPSTICKS
A chopstick can be very useful for manipulating the inside of a model, particularly to work on the detail and create points.

RULER
You can use different tools to help you fold and to make sure your proportions are accurate. You can use a ruler to create straight folds and to sharpen creases.

SCISSORS
A good, sharp pair of scissors is invaluable for cutting paper. The best for the task have long, straight cutting blades.

MAKING A SQUARE FROM A RECTANGLE

Always start with a true rectangle—all four corners must be 90 degrees.

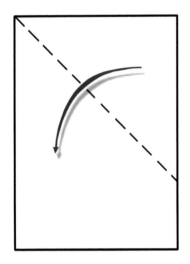

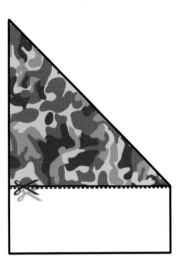

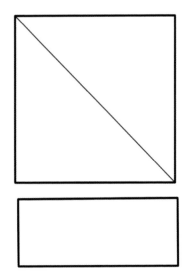

1 Fold the top edge of the paper diagonally so that the top edge aligns with the left-hand edge.

2 Fold the bottom edge of the paper up to the base of the triangle you have just made. Cut along this folded edge.

3 Unfold the triangle and the square is ready for use. You will have a square and a residual rectangle of paper.

MAKING A RECTANGLE FROM A SQUARE

Origami rectangles need to be of "A" proportions—A4, A3, A2. These stages show you how to get a rectangle of the correct proportions very simply from a sheet of square paper.

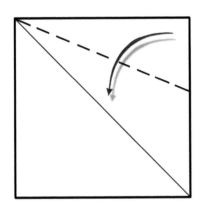

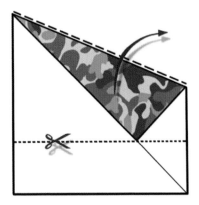

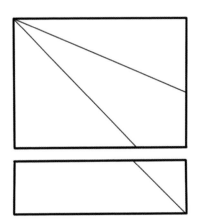

1 Fold the square in half diagonally and unfold. Now fold the top edge of your square so that it aligns with the diagonal crease.

2 Fold the lower edge of the paper up to the point at which the corner touches the diagonal crease. Cut along this crease.

3 Unfold the paper and a rectangle of the "A" proportions is ready for use. You will also have a residual rectangle.

9

BASIC TECHNIQUES

Although folding paper might seem the easiest of crafts, there are a few basic techniques to master before you can start. The construction process for each of the models in this book is illustrated using step diagrams. Alongside the diagrams you will find arrows and fold lines that show how a particular fold should be carried out. These are all explained on the following pages.

SYMBOLS

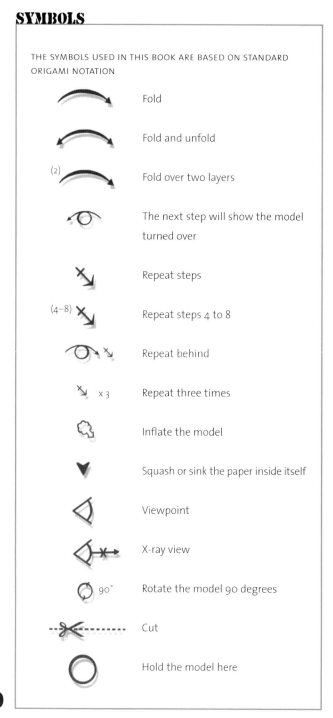

THE SYMBOLS USED IN THIS BOOK ARE BASED ON STANDARD ORIGAMI NOTATION

Fold

Fold and unfold

(2) Fold over two layers

The next step will show the model turned over

Repeat steps

(4–8) Repeat steps 4 to 8

Repeat behind

x 3 Repeat three times

Inflate the model

Squash or sink the paper inside itself

Viewpoint

X-ray view

90° Rotate the model 90 degrees

Cut

Hold the model here

BASIC FOLDS

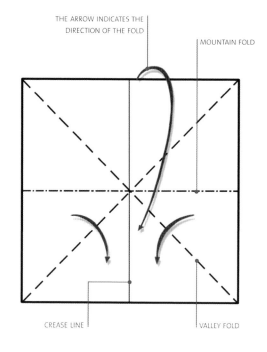

THE ARROW INDICATES THE DIRECTION OF THE FOLD

MOUNTAIN FOLD

CREASE LINE

VALLEY FOLD

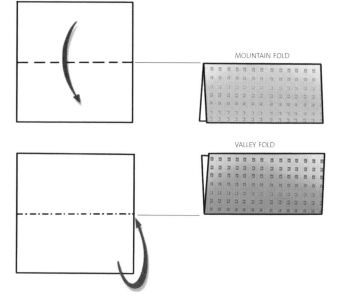

MOUNTAIN FOLD

VALLEY FOLD

FOLLOWING INSTRUCTIONS

The projects are broken down into a series of simple steps. Each step has a corresponding diagram that shows you how to make that step's folds.

Before attempting a step make sure that the model you have resembles the step diagram. Each diagram shows where to make each fold. The red arrows show the direction of the fold.

When you have completed a step, carefully look at the model to see if it resembles the next step. If your model does not look right, don't worry, just look closely at the instructions and try working back until you can match your model with an earlier step.

FOLDING TIPS

1	Follow the steps in numerical order, and fold one step at a time.
2	Look out for the reference points, both in the step you are trying to complete, but also by looking forward to see how the model should look when the fold is completed.
3	Fold as accurately as possible. If the step requires the model to be folded in half, fold and match the two edges of the model together and then make the crease.
4	You should fold on a flat, level surface. You can fold in the air, but it is easier to make clean accurate folds when working on a flat surface.
5	Make creases as sharply as possible. It may help to enhance the creases by running a fingernail or other object, such as a bone folder, along the folded edge.

FOLDING IN HALF

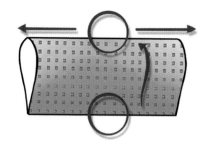

1 This diagram indicates that the square of paper should be folded in half.

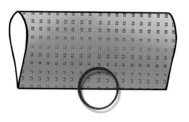

2 First of all line up the opposite edges and hold them together.

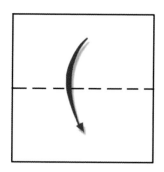

3 Now pinch at the center of the folded edge and make the crease, smoothing from the center out to the edges.

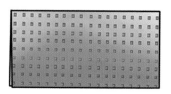

4 Keep holding the edges together as you sharpen the crease, the paper is now folded in half.

BASIC TECHNIQUES CONTINUED
REVERSE FOLD

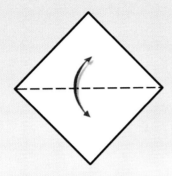

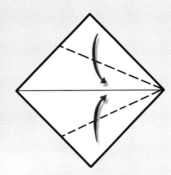

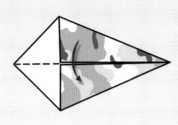

1 Fold and unfold the square of paper diagonally.

2 Fold the edges to the middle crease of the paper as shown.

3 Fold the model horizontally, along the middle.

4 This arrow indicates a reverse fold, along the dotted line.

5 This interim stage shows the point reversing into itself.

6 The reverse fold is now complete.

PRELIMINARY BASE

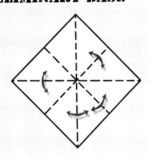

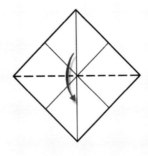

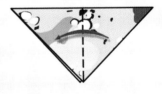

1 Fold and unfold the square in half horizontally, vertically, and diagonally.

2 Fold the square in half along one of the diagonal creases.

3 Fold in half again, along the center fold.

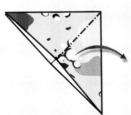

4 Slip a finger inside the top layer and lift the paper.

5 Squash the paper down to flatten the point.

6 Turn over and repeat steps 3 to 5. The preliminary base.

WATERBOMB BASE

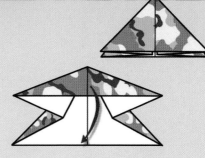

1 Fold and unfold the square in half horizontally, vertically, and diagonally.

2 Fold the square in half horizontally and reverse the folds in the diagonal creases.

3 Continue to fold and flatten the model, and it is complete.

BIRD BASE

Start with the completed preliminary base on page 12.

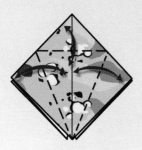

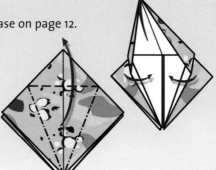

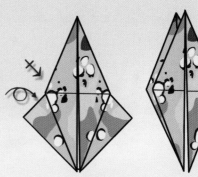

1 Fold and unfold the side edges and top corner, as shown.

2 Lift up the front layer and fold along the top crease. Fold in each of the sides.

3 Turn over and repeat steps 1 and 2 on the other side. The bird base is now complete.

FROG BASE

Start with the preliminary base on page 12.

1 Fold and unfold the side edge to the center crease.

2 Open the corner and flatten the paper along the new fold.

3 Fold and unfold the lower edges to the center crease.

4 Push the center section up and back. Refold the lower edges.

5 Repeat steps 1 to 4 on the other three points.

6 The frog base is complete and should look like this. **13**

BARGE

The ideal vessel for ferrying troops upstream, this camouflage **barge** is quick and easy to make. You will have a mini fleet in no time at all.

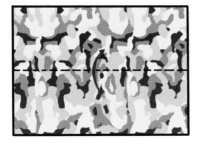

1 Start with a rectangle of paper, pattern-side up. Fold in half horizontally and unfold.

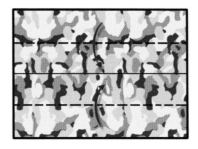

2 Fold the top and bottom edges in to meet the center crease.

3 Fold the bottom corners diagonally, as shown.

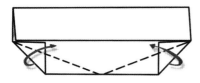

4 Follow the diagram to fold the corners again.

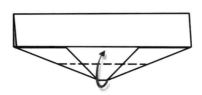

5 Bring the bottom edge up to meet the center line, as shown.

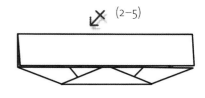

6 Now turn the model over and repeat the folds in steps 2 to 5 on the other side.

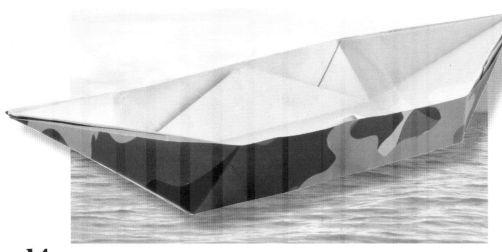

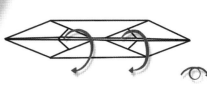

7 Turn the top layer inside out and turn the model over. The barge is now complete.

LANDING CRAFT

Need to get your troops and weapons from ship to shore? Here is the perfect landing craft, complete with an access ramp door.

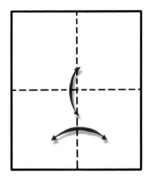 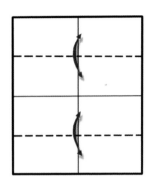 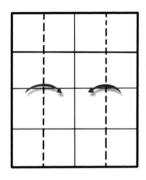

1 Pattern-side down, fold and unfold a rectangle horizontally and vertically.

2 Fold and unfold the short edges to the center.

3 Fold the long edges to meet the center crease.

4 Fold the corners to meet the center crease and unfold.

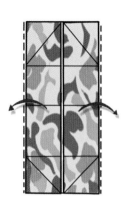

5 Now unfold the flaps to open the paper out flat.

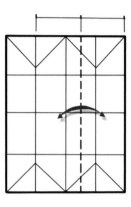

6 Fold and unfold one side between the center and quarter creases.

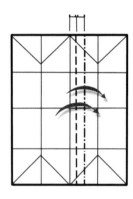

7 Fold the same edge over on the 7/16ths crease, and back again on the fold made in step 6.

(6–7)

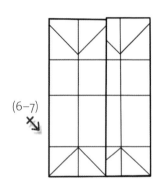

8 Repeat steps 6 and 7 on the other side.

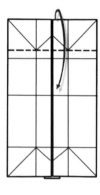

9 Fold the top edge over to the line indicated.

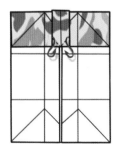

10 Fold the two inner corners underneath.

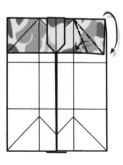

11 Open out the top right corner and squash flat along the diagonal fold.

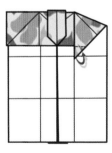

12 Fold the bottom corner underneath as shown.

16

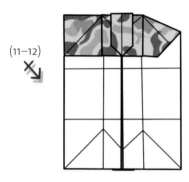

(11–12)

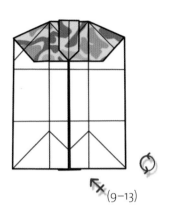

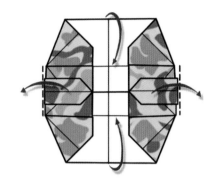

(9–13)

13 Repeat steps 11 and 12 on the left side.

14 Repeat steps 9 to 13 on the lower section of the model and rotate 90 degrees.

15 Lift and pull out the end flaps to open up the model.

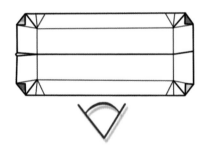

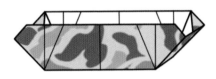

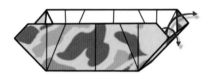

16 The model seen from above. The next step will show the side view.

17 The landing craft is complete, and should look like this.

18 To lower the ramp unfold the top corners as shown.

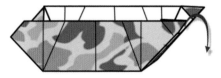

19 Now you can lower the ramp and let your troops off.

AIRCRAFT CARRIER

No navy is complete without its flagship aircraft carrier. There are plenty of folds to make so you need to be meticulous from the start.

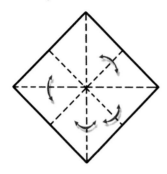 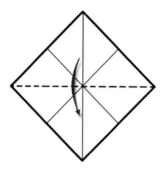 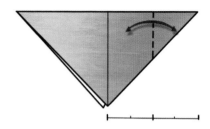

1 Pattern-side down, fold and unfold a square in half vertically, horizontally, and diagonally.

2 Fold the square in half diagonally.

3 Fold and unfold one corner to the center.

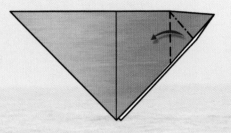

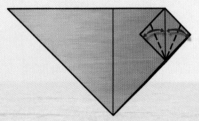

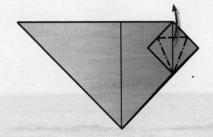

4 Squash the corner flat along the fold made in step 3.

5 Fold and unfold the edges into the center of the diamond you have made.

6 Fold up the front flap. This will cause the folds made in step 5 to reverse.

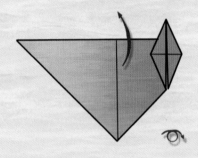

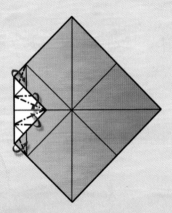

7 Unfold the model completely to open it flat.

8 Fold the left point along the line indicated above.

9 Refold the creases made in steps 5 to 7.

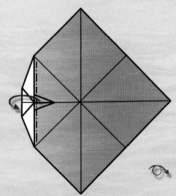

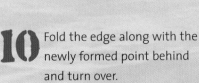

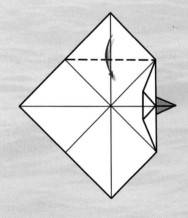

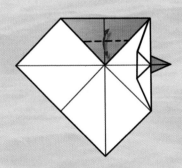

10 Fold the edge along with the newly formed point behind and turn over.

11 Fold the top point in to the center of the model.

12 Fold the point back on itself and unfold.

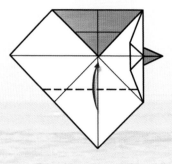 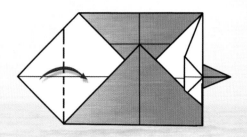 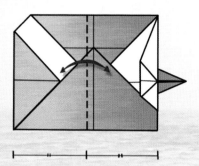

13 Fold the lower edge up to meet the crease made in the last step.

14 Fold the left-hand corner into the model, as shown.

15 Fold the model in half vertically and unfold.

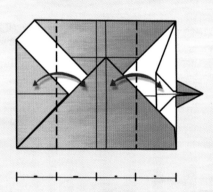 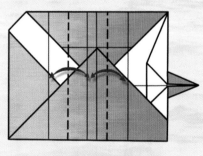 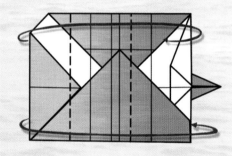

16 Fold and unfold the outer edges to the center crease.

17 Use the creases made in step 16 to fold and unfold the outer edges again, as shown.

18 Lift the left-hand edge and tuck it into the pocket in the right-hand edge.

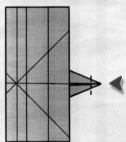 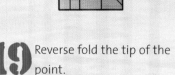 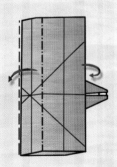 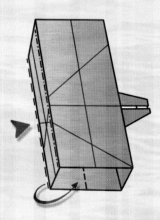

19 Reverse fold the tip of the point.

20 Reshape some of the folds to make a three-dimensional model.

21 Reverse fold the left-hand edge into the model.

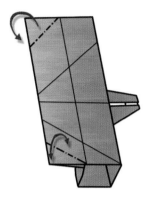

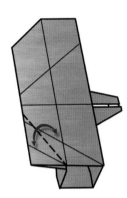

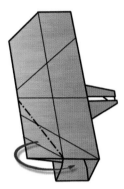

22 Fold over the back corner and fold and unfold the front corner.

23 Make a second fold in the front corner, as shown.

24 Reverse this last fold into the model.

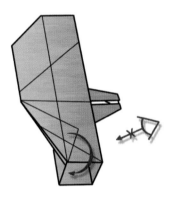

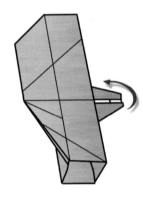

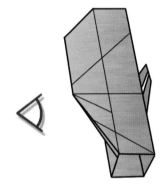

25 Fold down the triangle inside the model.

26 Fold the blunted point up to form the superstructure.

27 The next step shows a side view of the model.

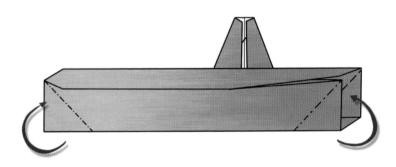

28 Reverse fold the front and back of the boat into the model, and it is complete.

SUBMARINE

Up periscope and prepare to surface with this sea-worthy submarine.
Although it has many steps, this is an easy vessel to make.

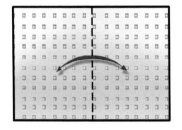

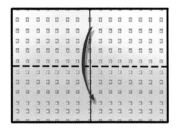

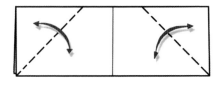

1 Pattern-side up, fold and unfold a rectangle in half vertically.

2 Carefully fold the rectangle in half horizontally.

3 Fold and unfold the corners, as shown above.

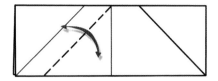

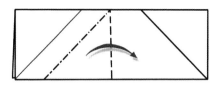

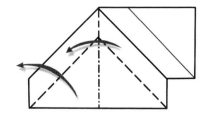

4 Make a second fold, bringing the left-hand edge to align with the center crease. Unfold.

5 Open out the left-hand corner and squash flat along the fold made in step 4.

6 Fold the flap back, reversing the fold made in step 3.

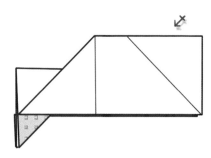

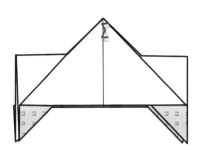

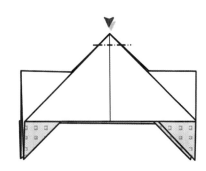

7 Repeat steps 4 to 6 on the other side of the model.

8 Fold and unfold about a third of the triangle.

9 Reverse the fold made in step 8 into the model.

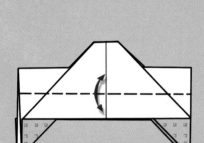

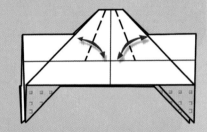

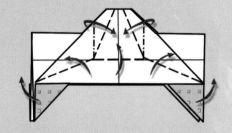

10 Fold and unfold the rectangle horizontally.

11 Fold and unfold between the edge of the triangle and the middle line.

12 Refold the folds made in steps 10 and 11. This will cause the lower triangles to fold out and flatten.

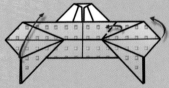

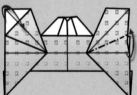

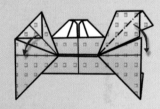

13 Fold the left-hand kite shape up. Lift the right-hand kite shape and roll it up the side.

14 Fold the left corner over. On the right side, reverse the lower triangle into the model.

15 Fold the left side down. Make the two folds on the right to roll the kite shape down.

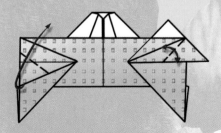

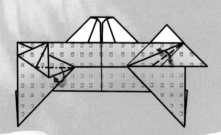

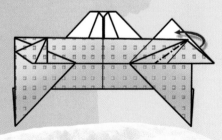

16 Fold the left corner up. Fold and unfold the corner on the right side, as shown.

17 Fold the bottom of the left corner into the model. On the right side make a second fold, as shown.

18 Reverse fold the right side of the model along the fold made in step 17.

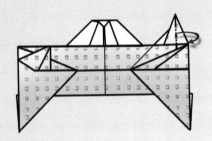 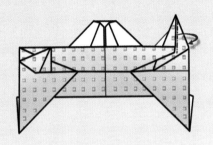 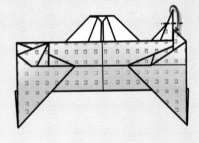

19 Fold the front flap of the triangle to the rear.

20 Now fold the lower flap of the triangle to the rear.

21 Reverse fold the top of the triangle.

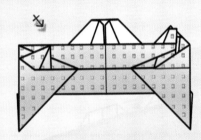 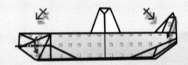

22 Turn the model over and repeat steps 10 to 21 on the other side.

23 Fold over the flaps on the hull and tail, on both sides. The submarine is complete.

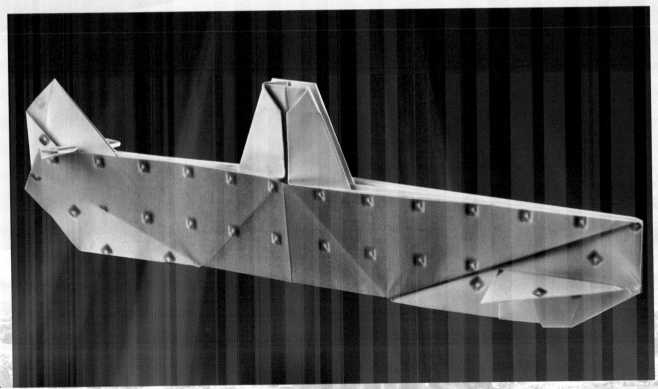

BATTLESHIP

Fun to assemble, this sturdy vessel is made from four separate components, a hull, a superstructure, and two gun turrets.

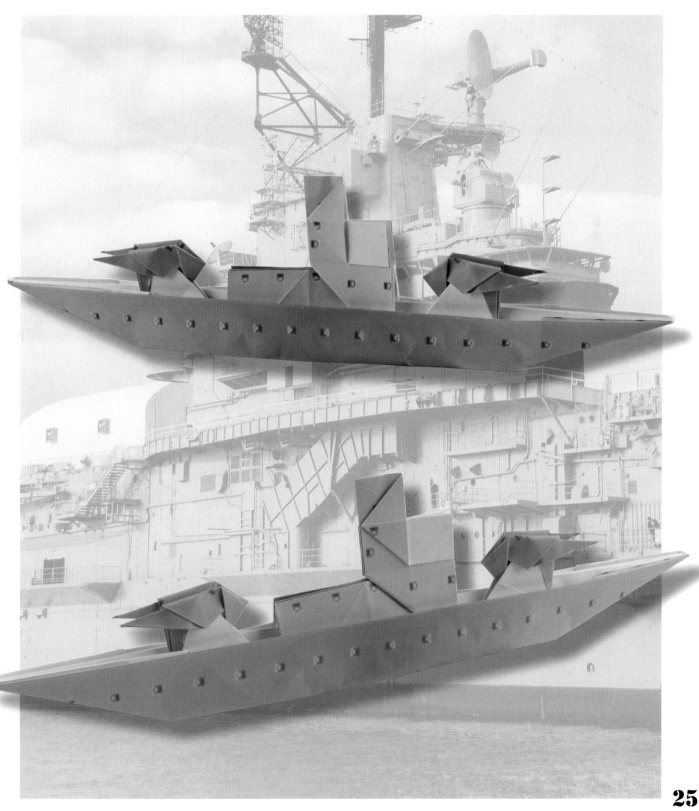

THE SUPERSTRUCTURE

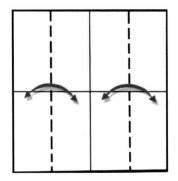

1 Pattern-side down, fold and unfold a square vertically and horizontally. Fold and unfold two edges to the center.

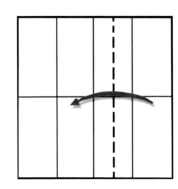

2 Fold the right-hand edge in to meet the quarter crease, as shown above.

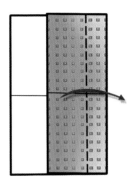

3 Now fold back again along the fold made in step 2.

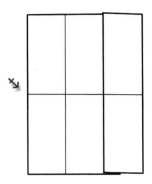

4 Repeat steps 2 and 3 on the left-hand side.

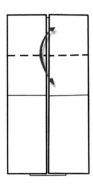

5 Fold and unfold the top edges to the middle.

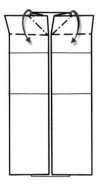

6 Holding the lower layer flat, fold the top layer down to meet the crease made in step 5.

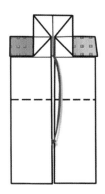

7 Fold the model in half, keeping it flat and square.

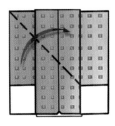

8 Fold the model in half diagonally as shown.

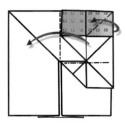

9 Fold the top layer back over. Lift the flap on the right. Push it to the left, opening and flattening the model as you go.

BATTLESHIP CONTINUED

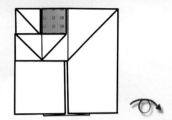

10 Now turn the model over again.

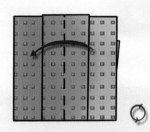

11 Fold the top layer in half vertically, and rotate 90 degrees counterclockwise.

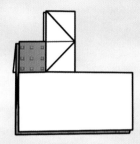

12 This is the bridge of your battleship, now complete.

THE GUN TURRETS

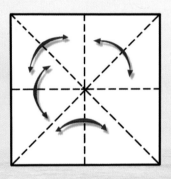

1 Pattern-side down, fold and unfold a square in half vertically horizontally, and diagonally.

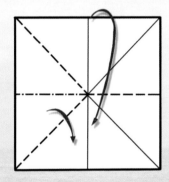

2 Fold the square in half and reverse the diagonal folds on the left-hand side.

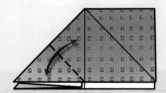

3 Fold the corner so that the bottom edge meets the center crease, as shown.

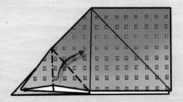

4 Open the point and carefully squash it flat along the fold made in step 3.

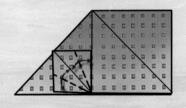

5 Fold and unfold the edges to the middle.

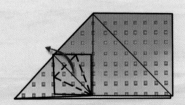

6 Fold up the front flap. This will cause the folds made in step 5 to reverse.

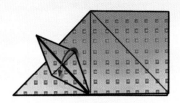

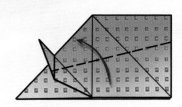

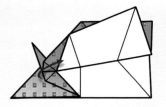

7 Fold the diamond shape accurately in half, as shown.

8 Fold the front layer up in the direction indicated.

9 Now fold the half diamond across from left to right.

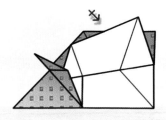

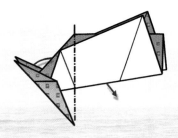

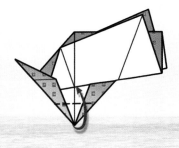

10 Repeat steps 3 to 9 on the other side of the model.

11 Fold the layer beneath from left to right, as shown.

12 Fold the corner up and into the model.

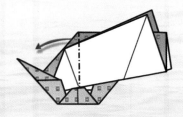

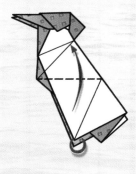

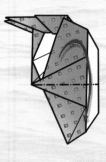

13 Fold the layer beneath back from the right to the left and rotate the model.

14 Fold the top layer up, while holding the layer beneath. The paper between the layers should be flat.

15 Now fold the bottom layer up as well.

BATTLESHIP CONTINUED

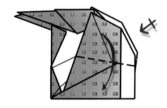

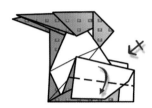

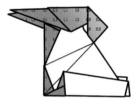

16 Fold the top layer over accurately.

17 Then fold the top layer over once more.

18 The gun turret is complete, repeat for the second gun.

THE HULL

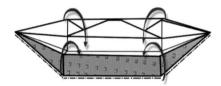

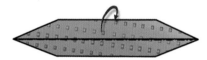

1 Starting with the completed barge (see page 76), fold the edges into the middle and flatten.

2 Now fold the model in half, horizontally.

3 The hull is now complete. You can now assemble the components as indicated below.

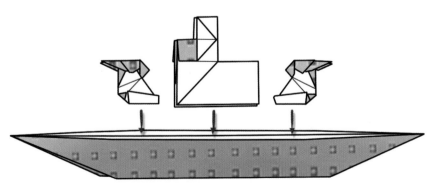

4 Place the bridge in the center of the hull, then place the gun turrets, one facing the bow and one the stern.

GLOSSARY

American Revolution (uh-MER-uh-ken reh-vuh-LOO-shun) Battles that soldiers from the colonies fought against Britain for freedom, from 1775 to 1783.

barge (BARJ) A boat with a flat bottom, used to carry goods on rivers.

fleet (FLEET) Many ships under the command of one person.

origami (or-uh-GAH-mee) The art of folding paper into decorative shapes or objects.

personnel (per-sun-EL) The people employed in any work, business, or service.

proportions (pruh-POR-shunz) Proper or equal shares.

reconnaissance (ree-CON-ih-sens) A survey, as of an enemy territory, to gain information.

submarine (SUB-muh-reen) A ship that is made to travel underwater.

techniques (tek-NEEKZ) Methods or ways of bringing about a desired result in a science, an art, a sport, or a profession.

FURTHER READING

Jackson, Kay. *Navy Ships in Action.* Amazing Military Vehicles. New York: PowerKids Press, 2009.

Nagle, Jeanne. *Navy.* US Military Forces. New York: Gareth Stevens Learning Library, 2011.

Yomtov, Nel. *Navy SEALs in Action.* Special Ops. New York: Bearport Publishing, 2008.

WEBSITES

Due to the changing nature of Internet links, PowerKids Press has developed an online list of websites related to the subject of this book. This site is updated regularly. Please use this link to access the list:
www.powerkids.com/orar/navy/

INDEX